Adversity Road

Author: Kendall T. Newell

Illustrator: Tionna J. Clarida

To order additional copies of this book, contact:
Xlibris
844-714-8691
www.Xlibris.com
Orders@Xlibris.com

ISBN: Softcover   979-8-3694-1767-6
        Hardcover   979-8-3694-1768-3
        EBook   979-8-3694-1766-9

Print information available on the last page

Rev. date: 03/20/2024

Kendall Newell

The author, Kendall Newell, started his career as an elementary teacher in 2018 where he took his passion into the classroom to encourage students to reach for the stars and to never lose sight of their dreams. His award-winning children's book, *A Star Upon a Dream*, is about not allowing people and circumstances to dictate what you can achieve in life. Despite the obstacles the author encountered on his adversity road, Kendall went on to earn his Bachelor of Arts in early childhood education from Heidelberg University. He earned his Master of Education in educational leadership from Concordia University and his K-6 principal's license from Wright State University. Kendall is working towards earning his educational specialist degree in curriculum & instruction from Liberty University. He could not have persevered through this journey without a strong support system consisting of family and teachers. The author is appreciative of their love and support over the years. Set your goals high. As long as there are stars in the night sky, there is no limit to what you can achieve. You are a star— a star upon a dream.

Kendall Newell

Special Thank You:
Amy Filc – Editor & Former Teacher of the Author & Mina Creamer – Graphic Designer

Tionna Clarida

With an unyielding wanderlust and immense love for nature, Tionna Clarida is a professional artist devoted to crafting intriguing landscapes that immerse the viewer alongside the visual journey. With a Bachelor in the Arts, she brings a unique perspective to each piece of artwork she creates. The breadth of her work spans from cartoons, realism, abstract, landscapes, portraits as well as 2D and 3D sculptures. Watercolor is her medium of choice but she is also partial to oil paint. A graduate from the University of Central Arkansas, Tionna is currently based in Little Rock, Arkansas originating from New York, NY. In addition to nature being a significant source of her inspiration, she also draws creativity from words, poetry and sightseeing. Another source of her inspiration comes from the love and support of her parents, Bernard & Catherine Clarida.

Tionna Jr. Clarida

Journey the road,
Adversity road.

1

The road brings challenges.
Challenges I have,
Challenges to overcome.

Experiences of failure,
Heart-breaking failure.

Feelings of hopelessness,
Heart-breaking hopelessness.

3

Through the struggle,
I endeavor.

Through the challenges,
I persevere.

Experiences of success,
Joyful success.

Feelings of hopefulness,
Joyful hopefulness.

5

The road brought challenges.
Challenges I had,
Challenges I overcame.

Journeyed the road,
Adversity road.

7

Traverse the road,
Adversity road.

9

The road brings trials.
Trials I have,
Trials to overcome.

Experiences of defeat,
tragic defeat.

Feelings of discouragement,
tragic discouragement.

Through the struggle,
I endeavor.

Through the challenges,
I persevere.

12

Experiences of victory,
Joyous victory.

Feelings of encouragement,
Joyous encouragement.

The road brought trials.
Trials I had,
Trials I overcame.

14

Traversed the road,
Adversity road.

I am resilient.

Navigate the road,
Adversity road.

The road brings obstacles.
Obstacles I have,
Obstacles to overcome.

18

Experiences of setbacks,
painful setbacks.

Feelings of inadequacy,
painful inadequacy.

Through the struggle,
I endeavor.

Through the challenges,
I persevere.

20

Experiences of accomplishment,
heart-felt accomplishment.

Feelings of sufficiency,
heart-felt sufficiency.

The road brought obstacles.
Obstacles I had,
Obstacles I overcame.

22

Navigated the road,
Adversity road.

I am resilient.

24

You have challenges to face.
Trials to conquer,
Obstacles to overcome.

With your resilience,

You can face your challenges.
Conquer your trials,
Overcome your obstacles.

25

Through the struggle,
we endeavor.

Through the challenges,
we persevere.

You are never alone because together we walk the road,

The adversity road.

27

Printed in the United States
by Baker & Taylor Publisher Services